SAN PABLO

Cold Case FILE
Murder in the Mountains

by Olivia Gordon

Consultant: Dr. John P. Cassella
Principal Lecturer in Forensic Science
Staffordshire University, England

BEARPORT
New York, New York

Credits

Cover, © Pogosova Anna Grigorievna/Shutterstock, © Vasiliy Koval/Shutterstock, and © Gunnison County, Colorado, Sheriff's Office; Title Page, © Gunnison County, Colorado, Sheriff's Office; 4, © Shutterstock; 5, © Gunnison County, Colorado, Sheriff's Office; 6, © Tracy Morgan/Dorling Kindersley; 7T, © Motoring Picture Library; 7B, © Gunnison County, Colorado, Sheriff's Office; 8, © Andy Holligan/DK Images; 9L, © Gunnison County, Colorado, Sheriff's Office; 9R, © Mikael Karlsson/Arrestimgimages.com; 10T, © Gunnison County, Colorado, Sheriff's Office; 10B, © Shutterstock; 11T, © Pascal Goetgheluck/Science Photo Library; 11B, © Steve Gschmeissner/Science Photo Library; 12, © Gunnison County, Colorado, Sheriff's Office; 13L, © Jim West/Alamy; 13R, © NecroSearch; 14, © Marc Dietrich/Big White Box; 15, © Mauro Fermariello/Science Photo Library; 16T, © Arthur Gurmankin/Big White Box; 16BL, © Greg Boiarsky/Big White Box; 16BR, © Shutterstock; 17, © Science Photo Library; 18, © Gunnison County, Colorado, Sheriff's Office; 19T, © Greg Boiarsky/Big White Box; 19B, © John Powell/Rex Features; 20, © Pascal Goetgheluck/Science Photo Library; 21, © Gunnison County, Colorado, Sheriff's Office; 22L, © Gunnison County, Colorado, Sheriff's Office; 22R, © Gunnison County, Colorado, Sheriff's Office; 23B, © Rex Features; 24, © Gunnison County, Colorado, Sheriff's Office; 25T, © Gunnison County, Colorado, Sheriff's Office; 25B, © brandXpictures; 28, © Stefan Klein/istockphoto; 29, © Rex Features; 30, © Louise Murray/Alamy.

Every effort has been made by ticktock Entertainment Ltd. to trace copyright holders. We apologize in advance for any omissions. We would be pleased to insert the appropriate acknowledgments in any subsequent edition of this publication.

Publisher: Kenn Goin
Editorial Director: Adam Siegel
Project Editor: Dinah Dunn
Creative Director: Spencer Brinker
Original Design: ticktock Entertainment Ltd.

Library of Congress Cataloging-in-Publication Data

Gordon, Olivia.
 Cold case file : murder in the mountains / by Olivia Gordon.
    p. cm. — (Crime solvers)
 Includes bibliographical references and index.
 ISBN-13: 978-1-59716-547-1 (lib. bdg.)
 ISBN-10: 1-59716-547-6 (lib. bdg.)
 1. Wallace, Michele, d. 1974. 2. Melanson, Roy. 3. Murder—Investigation—Colorado—Juvenile literature. 4. Cold cases (Criminal investigation)—Colorado—Juvenile literature. 5. Murder—Colorado—Juvenile literature. 6. Missing persons—Colorado—Juvenile literature. I. Title.

HV8079.H6G67 2008
364.152'3092—dc22
                                    2007023539

Contents

A Disappearance

Michele Wallace was an adventurous young photographer. She was excited when she called her family in August 1974. She was about to set off with her dog, Okee, for a short camping trip in the Rocky Mountains.

There was little reason to worry about her safety. "She was a tough little cookie," recalled her father, George. "She climbed mountains, jumped out of airplanes, and roped cattle."

Michele spent the summer photographing the spectacular Colorado landscape.

At the end of her trip, on August 30, 1974, Michele came across two men sitting in a battered car. They were Chuck Matthews, a local **ranch hand** who owned the car, and Roy Melanson, a **drifter**. They offered to give Michele a ride back to her car. She and Okee climbed in.

By the time they reached Michele's car, Matthews's car had broken down. So Michele drove the two men into town.

Chuck Matthews got out and thanked Michele. Then Matthews heard Roy Melanson ask Michele for a ride to his car. Matthews thought that was strange. Melanson had told him he did not have a car.

FACT FILE

The Crime

Victim:
Michele Wallace, a photographer living in Gunnison County, Colorado

Age:
25 years old

Motive:
Unknown

Date of Crime:
August 30, 1974

Location:
The Rocky Mountains, Colorado

Michele Wallace

The Search

When Michele did not return from her camping trip, her family grew worried. On September 2, they contacted the police, who launched a huge search party.

Four hundred volunteers spent thousands of hours searching more than 2,100 square miles (5,439 sq km). They found no trace of Michele or her car. Her dog, Okee, was found. He had been shot by a rancher for bothering his cattle.

Michele's dog was later found dead.

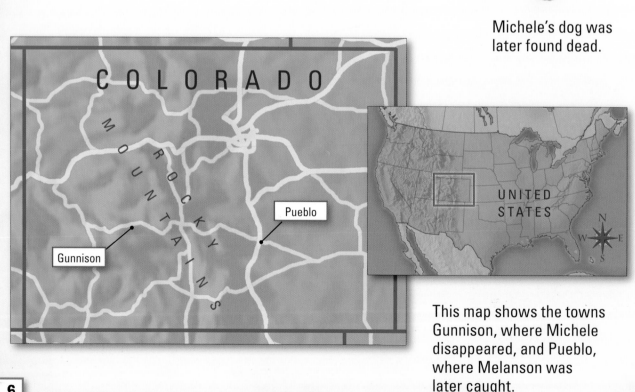

This map shows the towns Gunnison, where Michele disappeared, and Pueblo, where Melanson was later caught.

During this time, Chuck Matthews heard a news report about a missing 25-year-old woman. He immediately called the **sheriff**'s department. He told them about meeting Michele and Roy Melanson's strange request for a ride.

Roy Melanson drove to Pueblo in Michele's Mazda station wagon.

Police caught up with Melanson less than two weeks later in Pueblo, Colorado. He was driving Michele's car. He had **pawned** Michele's camping gear and camera. When her camera was recovered, it showed that the last photo Michele took was of Melanson.

FACT FILE

The Prime Suspect: Roy Melanson

The case against Melanson:

- Last person to see Michele alive
- Lied to Michele about having a car
- Wanted by police for attacking other women
- Had taken Michele's possessions
- The last photo from the film in Michele's camera was a shot of Melanson.

Murder suspect Roy Melanson

The Case Goes Cold

Roy Melanson admitted to taking Michele's belongings but claimed he had not hurt her. He said Michele had let him borrow her car and he had dropped her off at a bar. The police suspected him of murder. Without a body, however, they were unable to **prosecute** him.

Michele's mother, Maggie, struggled with the loss of her daughter. Five weeks after Michele's disappearance, Maggie killed herself. In the note she left behind, she asked that her daughter's body be buried next to hers when it was found. Her father, George, and brother, George Jr., struggled on.

Hikers in the Rockies discovered an important clue.

For five long years, the case remained unsolved. Then, in 1979, some hikers in the mountains made an awful discovery. They found a human **scalp** with two long brown braids the same color as Michele's.

With this new evidence, the case was reopened. Unfortunately, at the time, investigators did not have the **technology** to prove the scalp was Michele's. They searched the area near where the scalp was found but did not find any other **remains**.

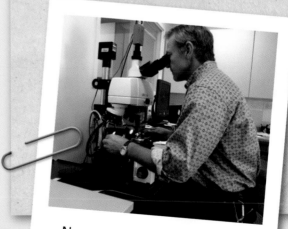

New technology helps police solve cold cases.

The scalp found by hikers in 1979

The Detective

In 1989, a new **investigator** joined the Gunnison County sheriff's office. Kathy Young took an interest in Michele's case. She examined the most recent clues, including the scalp with the braids. She also found Michele's hairbrush, which had been collected from her home at the time of the disappearance.

Sheriff Rick Murdie agreed to let Kathy Young work on the cold case.

Young sent the scalp and hairbrush to the Colorado Bureau of Investigation for forensic **analysis**. The laboratory's Hair and Fiber Analysis team compared the hairs from the scalp and the brush. The team believed that they were from the same person.

Hair from Michele's brush matched the hair from the scalp found in the mountains.

Young dug further into the case. She visited Roy Melanson who was now in a Kentucky prison. He was awaiting trial for another possible crime— robbery. He refused to talk to her about the case.

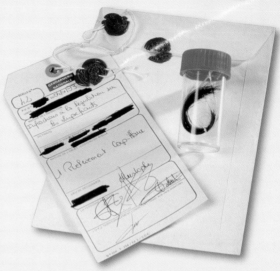

A hair sample ready for analysis

Young spoke with other prisoners who shared his cell. They said he had boasted of killing a woman in Colorado. Young now had more evidence, but was it enough to charge Melanson with murder?

This is what hair looks like under a microscope.

FACT FILE

Hair Analysis: Part One

- The Hair and Fiber laboratory team at the Colorado Bureau of Investigation analyzes human and animal hairs, bones, and fibers, such as thread used in clothing.

- When testing hair, scientists put strands on a glass slide and examine them under a **microscope**. They test the strands to determine the age, **gender**, and race of the person.

- Using a microscope, forensic scientists can match hairs from the same head found in different places. This is what the Colorado Bureau of Investigation lab did in Michele's case.

Getting Away with Murder?

The sheriff's department decided that they had enough evidence to charge Roy Melanson with murder. Melanson's lawyer disagreed—the police didn't even have Michele's body.

The sheriff's department was concerned. It is against the law to **try** a person more than once for the same crime. They had only one chance to send Melanson to prison for the death of Michele. Young continued to investigate every possible **lead**. She had to find Michele's body.

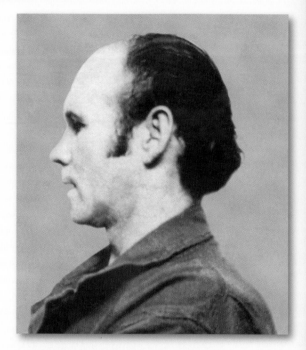

Roy Melanson knew the police had not found Michele's body.

A lab worker from the Hair and Fiber Analysis team told Young about an organization called NecroSearch that might help. It specialized in finding bodies buried in hidden **graves**. In October 1991, Young went to Denver to present her case to them.

"I really never believed we'd find anything," Young said. Yet she wanted to be sure her department had done all they could before taking Melanson to court.

NecroSearch members are skilled in finding bodies buried in hidden graves.

NecroSearch

Young was smart to approach NecroSearch. They had a remarkable team of experts from different scientific and investigative backgrounds. The members had a lot of success finding bodies.

The group's president, Jack Swanburg, was understandably proud of his team. He said that if you put the members together, "you've got a supersleuth that's going to be hard to beat."

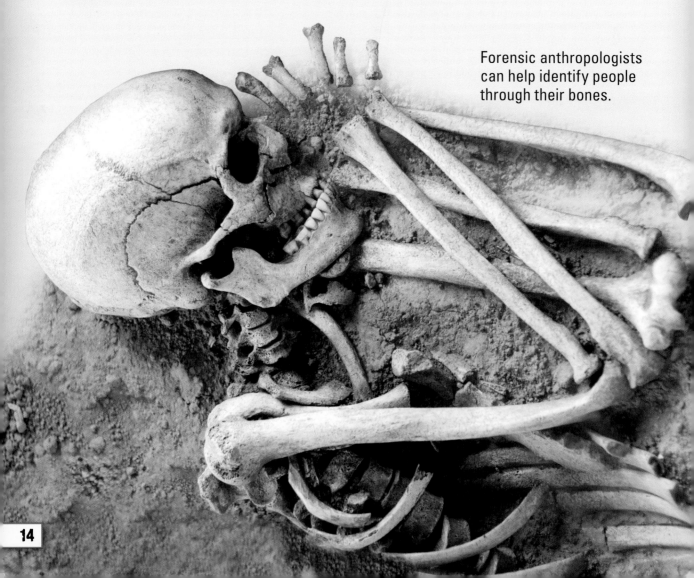

Forensic anthropologists can help identify people through their bones.

The members of NecroSearch use forensic methods to examine cases. They also personally help search for bodies. They use tools that range from ground-penetrating **radar** to dogs to just noticing when something seems out of place.

"If it just looks weird, maybe it's a place we want to investigate," said Diane France, a member of NecroSearch. The extra expertise they bring to a case often produces results that police won't find on their own.

FACT FILE
Calling In the Experts

Kathy Young knew she needed help finding Michele's body. NecroSearch was a good choice. Their team includes:

- *Forensic anthropologists*, who study human bones and can help determine the identity of a skeleton.

- *Animal trackers*, who study how wild animals behave. They can figure out where animals may have scattered the bones of a **victim**.

- *Forensic botanists*, who are plant experts. They can tell where a piece of evidence may have rested by examining small pieces of plants that were found with the evidence.

NecroSearch uses dogs specially trained to find dead bodies.

A New Search

In late fall of 1991, NecroSearch began working on Michele's case. Botanist Vickey Trammell examined the scalp. She noted that the hair had been lightened by the sun. So perhaps the body had not been buried.

The hair contained needles from fir trees. Trammell knew that this type of tree grows on the northern **slope** of the Rocky Mountains. This information helped NecroSearch determine where they would begin looking.

Fir needles were found in Michele's hair.

The Rocky Mountains could not be searched in the winter because they were covered in snow.

Unfortunately, the Rockies were covered with snow. So the search had to wait until the following summer.

On August 5, 1992, three volunteers from NecroSearch, as well as Kathy Young and other police officers, drove to Gunnison. They began a huge search. A day passed. They found nothing. Was Michele's body really out there?

FACT FILE

Hair Analysis: Part Two

- Since the mid-1990s, scientists have been able to analyze the **DNA** in hair, improving their chances of identifying who the hair belongs to.

- When other materials are found in hair, it can help investigators figure out where a person has been. In Michele's case, bits of plants in the braids pointed searchers to the north-facing slopes of the Rockies.

- Hair analysis can also show whether hair was pulled out in a struggle.

Scientists can discover a surprising amount from a small sample of hair.

Investigators searched the mountain slopes.

A Skull

After another morning of searching, the team was still empty-handed. During a break in the afternoon, Young considered giving up. NecroSearch's animal tracker Cecilia Travis kept looking. She worked her way down one of the slopes

Large white mushrooms dotted the ground. One that looked like a skull caught her eye. She went to move it so it wouldn't mislead other searchers.

A ray of light through the trees hit the mushroom. It gleamed! Travis suddenly realized she was holding a skull with a gold tooth in the jaw.

Michele Wallace's skull was found lying in the grass. The bottom jaw was missing.

"I knew I had Michele," Travis said. The skull was taken to a laboratory. Forensic dentists compared the skull to Michele's dental records. They matched. After 18 years of waiting, Michele Wallace was finally found.

White mushrooms like this one grow on the slopes of the Rockies.

FACT FILE
Forensic Dentists

- Forensic dentists help identify dead bodies when the victims' faces are unrecognizable.

- They note the shape and position of the teeth. They also note anything unusual, such as fillings or braces. Such items are compared to old X-rays or dental records of the victim.

- If there are no dental records, a victim's photograph is compared to the teeth to see if they are the same.

- Forensic dentists can sometimes identify a person from a single tooth.

- Forensic dentists are especially helpful in cold cases because teeth, which are made of bone, **decompose** slower than other body parts.

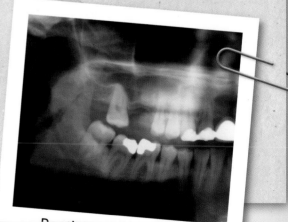

Dentists keep records of their patients' teeth, which may be used to identify them.

Gathering Evidence

Searchers returned to the Rockies. They spent the next few days on their hands and knees. They carefully combed the steep slope using a search grid. They spent the most time between the logging road where the scalp had been found and the location of the skull.

The dotted yellow lines in this picture show how a search grid divides an area into squares.

The team searched the area hoping to recover what was left of Michele. They found buttons, a boot, and orange thread in the grass. Most important they found 40 of Michele's bones. These included six ribs, two thigh bones, and 25 bones from one of her feet.

There wasn't enough evidence to say how Michele had been killed. Yet finding parts of her body helped build the case against Melanson.

Michele's left boot was found with the bones of her foot still inside.

Search Grids

To look for Michele's body, searchers used a technique called a search grid. First, the crime scene is divided into small squares. Searchers then examine each square before moving to the next one.

Other search patterns investigators use include:

Straight-line search: The search party walks side-by-side in a straight line, looking for anything unusual. If something is found, the line stops while the evidence is collected.

Spiral search: The search begins in a small circle in the center of the crime scene. It continues in larger circles until the whole crime scene is covered.

Strip search: This method is used when a small number of people have to search a large area. They cover it in straight lines, walking back and forth.

The Truth at Last

A forensic anthropologist studied the new evidence. Based on the location of the bones, she determined that Michele's body had been thrown from the road. It had rolled 25 feet (7.6 m) down the slope and stopped when it hit a tree.

This information helped prove that Michele had not died accidentally. Someone had killed her. All the clues pointed to Roy Melanson.

Michele Wallace

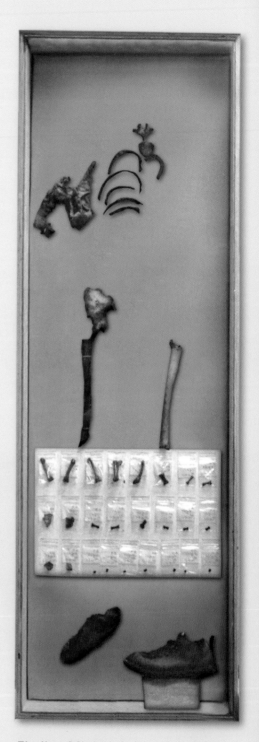

Finding Michele's bones helped prove she was murdered.

Michele's father couldn't believe that his daughter's body had been found. "After weeks and months and years, you give up all hope," he said. After all of these years, he was finally able to bury Michele beside her mother.

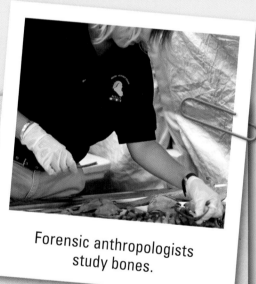

Forensic anthropologists study bones.

FACT FILE

Forensic Anthropology

- The science of examining the skeleton, or the bones of a dead body, is called forensic anthropology.

- A forensic anthropologist analyzes a person's bones to identify the victim. Bones can reveal a person's age, height, gender, race, medical history, and cause of death.

- The anthropologist in Michele's case determined that the bones belonged to a 25-year-old woman missing since 1974. There wasn't enough evidence, however, to determine how she had been killed.

The Court Case

In 1993, after nearly 20 years, Roy Melanson was finally tried in court for the murder of Michele Wallace. As part of the trial, the jury was taken to the site where Michele's bones had been found. There they could see what investigators think had happened in 1974. Chuck Matthews also told them about Melanson driving off with Michele and lying about having a car.

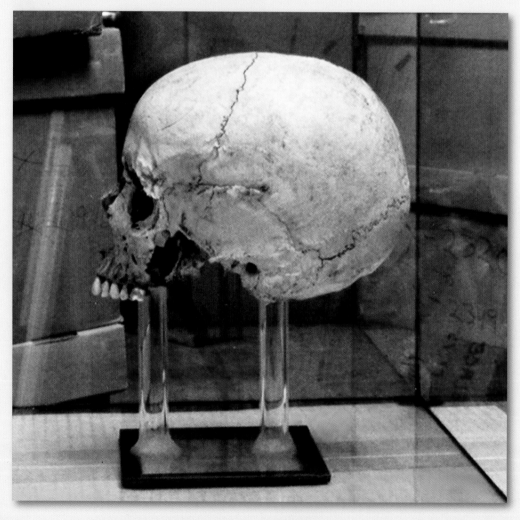

Michele's skull was an important piece of evidence.

The jury discussed the case for five and a half hours. They found Roy Melanson guilty of murder.

The judge **sentenced** Melanson to life in prison. Michele's father said, "Even though it takes a lot of time to accept, it does bring closure. And I know her mother's happy."

Roy Melanson was found guilty of Michele's murder.

FACT FILE

What Happened Next?

- Kathy Young joined NecroSearch as an investigator in 1993.

- Michele's father, George Wallace, was murdered in 2006.

- NecroSearch has helped solve hundreds of cases. They recently searched for the bodies of two children in Pennsylvania whom police believe were murdered 50 years ago.

- Roy Melanson is up for **parole** in 2012.

Roy Melanson's life sentence could last as little as 19 years.

Case Closed

August 30, 1974

Michele Wallace, a 25-year-old photographer, vanishes in the wilderness of the Rocky Mountains. She is last seen giving a ride to a drifter named Roy Melanson.

September 2, 1974

Michele Wallace's family contacts the police to report her missing. Volunteers search the mountains for her but find nothing.

September 12, 1974

The police arrest Roy Melanson in Pueblo, Colorado. He has Michele's car and receipts from selling her belongings.

July 26, 1979

Mountain hikers stumble on a scalp with two braids. The hair color is the same as Michele's. Police again search for Michele's body but find nothing.

1989

Kathy Young joins the Gunnison County sheriff's office. The Michele Wallace case is reopened. The scalp is confirmed as being Michele's. A new search is soon underway.

1991

Detective Kathy Young calls in experts from an organization called NecroSearch.

August 1992

Michele's skull and then 40 of her bones are discovered in the mountains. Forensic evidence shows she had been thrown down a slope from the road.

August 23, 1993

Roy Melanson's trial begins.

September 1, 1993

Roy Melanson is found guilty of murdering Michele Wallace. He is sentenced to life in prison.

Crime Solving Up Close

Cold Cases

Many criminal cases remain unsolved because there are no clues pointing to who committed the crime. If a long time passes without finding new evidence, then the case is considered cold.

- In the United States, more than one third of all murder cases are never solved.

- The longer a case lies cold, the less likely it is ever to be solved. In New York, for example, if a case has been cold for two years, it has less than a one percent chance of being solved.

- The most famous cold case is the murder of at least five women in London, England, in 1888. Two police forces worked together to try to catch the killer called "Jack the Ripper." They never found enough evidence to charge anyone with the crime.

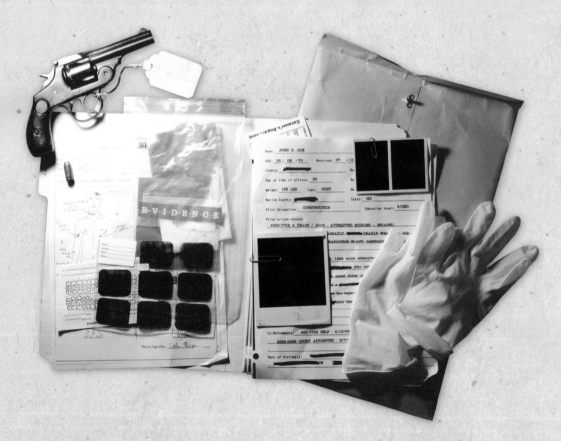

The police review a victim's file when they get new evidence.

Bone Detectives

Forensic anthropologists are scientists who study bones. They often work with investigators to help identify people based on their bones.

- In their laboratory, forensic anthropologists use a number of tests to analyze bones. These help figure out the age, height, health, gender, and race of the victim. Any identifying scars, such as broken bones that have healed, also are noted.

- Sometimes an artist works with the anthropologist to draw a picture or create a sculpture of how the person might have looked before he or she died. Police also use these images to help identify the victim.

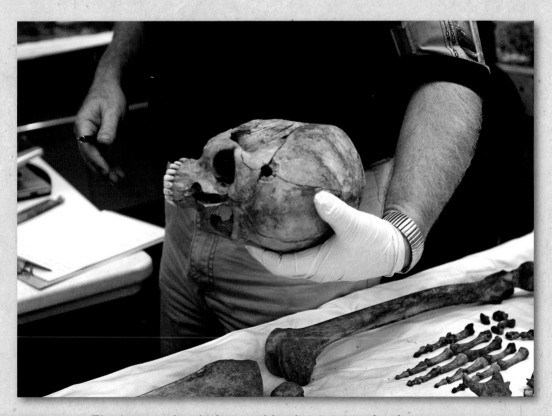

The bones of a victim provide clues as to who they were.

Crime Solving Up Close

Finding a Body

Since it began in 1987, NecroSearch has worked on more than 300 cases in six countries. Solving the murder of Michele Wallace was one of its first success stories. How does NecroSearch look for bodies?

- NecroSearch often uses ground-penetrating radar. This equipment is normally used to find things such as damaged underground pipes.

- The radar does not tell where bodies are buried. It shows where the ground has been disturbed, which can lead to finding a body.

- New NecroSearch workers practice using ground-penetrating radar by looking for dead pigs that have been buried on the grounds of a police training facility.

High-tech equipment, like this ground-penetrating radar, can help locate bodies.

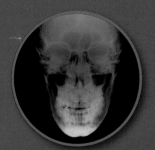

Glossary

analysis (uh-NAL-uh-siss) a detailed examination

clues (KLOOZ) objects or information that make it easier for a person to solve a mystery

decompose (dee-kuhm-POZE) to rot or break down

DNA (DEE EN AY) the molecule that carries the code for a living thing

drifter (DRIFT-uhr) a person who doesn't live in one place for long

evidence (EV-uh-duhnss) objects or information that can be used to prove whether something is true

forensic (fuh-REN-sik) using science and technology to help solve crimes

gender (JEN-der) being either male or female

graves (GRAYVZ) holes dug into the ground where dead people are buried

investigator (in-VESS-tuh-*gate*-ur) detective

lead (LEED) a piece of useful advice or information

microscope (MYE-kruh-*skope*) a tool that scientists use to see things that are too small to see with their eyes alone

parole (puh-ROLE) an early release of a prisoner

pawned (PAWND) to leave an item at a store in exchange for a cash loan

prosecute (PROSS-uh-kyoot) to carry out legal action in court against someone accused of a crime

radar (RAY-dar) a system that finds solid objects by bouncing radio waves off of them

ranch hand (RANCH HAND) a person who works on a cattle or horse farm

remains (ri-MAYNZ) all or part of a dead body

scalp (SKALP) the skin on the top of the head, including the hair

sentenced (SEN-tuhnsst) given time in jail as punishment for a crime

sheriff (SHER-if) the person in charge of enforcing the law in a county

slope (SLOHP) steep angle

technology (tek-NOL-uh-jee) the use of science to do practical things

try (TRYE) to put a person accused of a crime on trial

victim (VIK-tuhm) a person who is hurt or killed

Index

Read More

Hunter, William. *Mark and Trace Analysis.* Broomall, PA: Mason Crest Publishers (2005).

Jackson, Donna M. *Bone Detectives: How Forensic Anthropologists Solve Crimes and Uncover Mysteries of the Dead.* New York: Little, Brown & Company (1996).

Libal, Angela. *Forensic Anthropology.* Broomall, PA: Mason Crest Publishers (2005).

Learn More Online

To learn more about crime solving and the Michele Wallace case, visit
www.bearportpublishing.com/CrimeSolvers

About the Author

Olivia Gordon is a freelance journalist and writer who lives in London. Her nonfiction has appeared in papers and magazines including the *Telegraph*, the *Observer*, and the *Guardian*.